SCOTLAND

GALLERY BOOKS
An Imprint of W. H. Smith Publishers Inc.
112 Madison Avenue
New York City 10016

This edition first published in U.S.
in 1991 by Gallery Books,
an imprint of W.H. Smith Publishers, Inc.
112 Madison Avenue, New York, New York 10016

ISBN 0-8317-0254-0

Printed and bound in Spain

For rights information about the photographs in
this book please contact:

The Image Bank
111 Fifth Avenue, New York, NY 10003

Producer: Solomon M. Skolnick
Writer: Erin Hennessey
Design Concept: Lesley Ehlers
Designer: Ann-Louise Lipman
Editor: Sara Colacurto
Production: Valerie Zars
Photo Researcher: Edward Douglas
Assistant Photo Researcher: Robert V. Hale
Editorial Assistant: Carol Raguso

Title page: The massed pipes and brass of the Scottish Highland Brigade are a continuing symbol of Scotland's proud heritage. *Opposite:* Princes Street, Edinburgh's main thoroughfare, is bathed in evening light in a view from nearby Calton Hill.

To say that Scotland has a dramatic history is like saying haggis is a bit filling. Haggis, for the uninitiated, is a Scottish dish, consisting of a boiled mixture of the pluck (heart, liver, and lungs) of a sheep, oatmeal, and onions. It is traditionally served on Burns' birthday, which is remembered on January 25th in a lavish meal that includes cock-a-leekie soup and tatties-an-neeps (potatoes and turnips).

Haggis has a strong flavor and is not for the faint of heart. Neither is Scotland. The Scots can chart their history back to the Stone Age. Tribal warfare, endless invasions, and treachery in high places are all part of its colorful history. And what a hoary and complex history it is. Ancient dwellings and mysterious cairns (stone markers) like the Standing Stones of Callanish on the Isle of Lewis in the Outer Hebrides serve as a reminder that Scotland's story is long and tumultuous—it covers 6,000 years of human existence.

The earliest settlers came by sea and by land. Some traveled north from England, while others came by boat from Ireland, Scandinavia, and the European continent. Even today it's possible to discern the different cultural traits that Scots have inherited from their ancestors.

Lowland Scots, for example, are of Anglo-Saxon descent, sharing a common ancestry with the English, while west coast Scots have links with the Irish. Then there are the Norse Scots, who inhabit the northeast reaches of the mainland and the Orkney and Shetland Islands.

Edinburgh Castle, located on the site of an extinct volcano, towers above the city.

Day or night, Edinburgh Castle is visible from most points in the city. *Below:* Between bustling, modern Princes Street and Edinburgh's ancient castle lies the tranquillity of the Princes Street Gardens.

As home of the Scottish National War Memorial, Edinburgh Castle maintains an active military presence. *Below:* Mons Meg, a fifteenth-century cannon on the battlements of Edinburgh Castle, was once described as a "great iron murderer."

This page: Stone-built and solid, the beautifully restored homes of Ramsay Gardens cling to the hillside next to Edinburgh Castle.

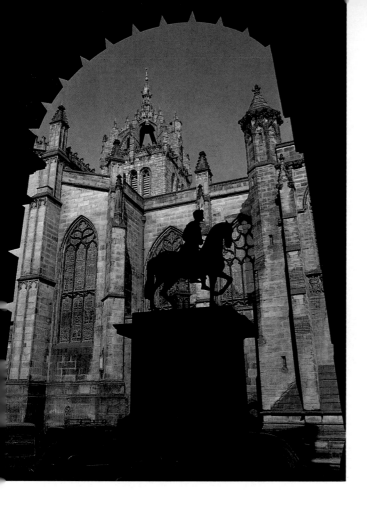
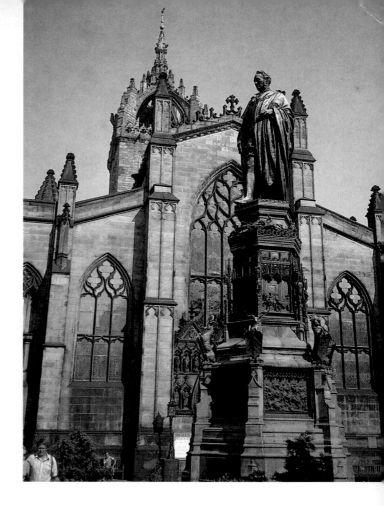

Above: A statue of King Charles II (left) dominates the entrance to Parliament Square and St. Giles Cathedral in Edinburgh's Old Town. St. Giles Cathedral (right), dedicated in the thirteenth century, is properly known as the High Kirk of Edinburgh. *Below:* Carefully restored, St. Giles is famous for its open-crowned steeple.

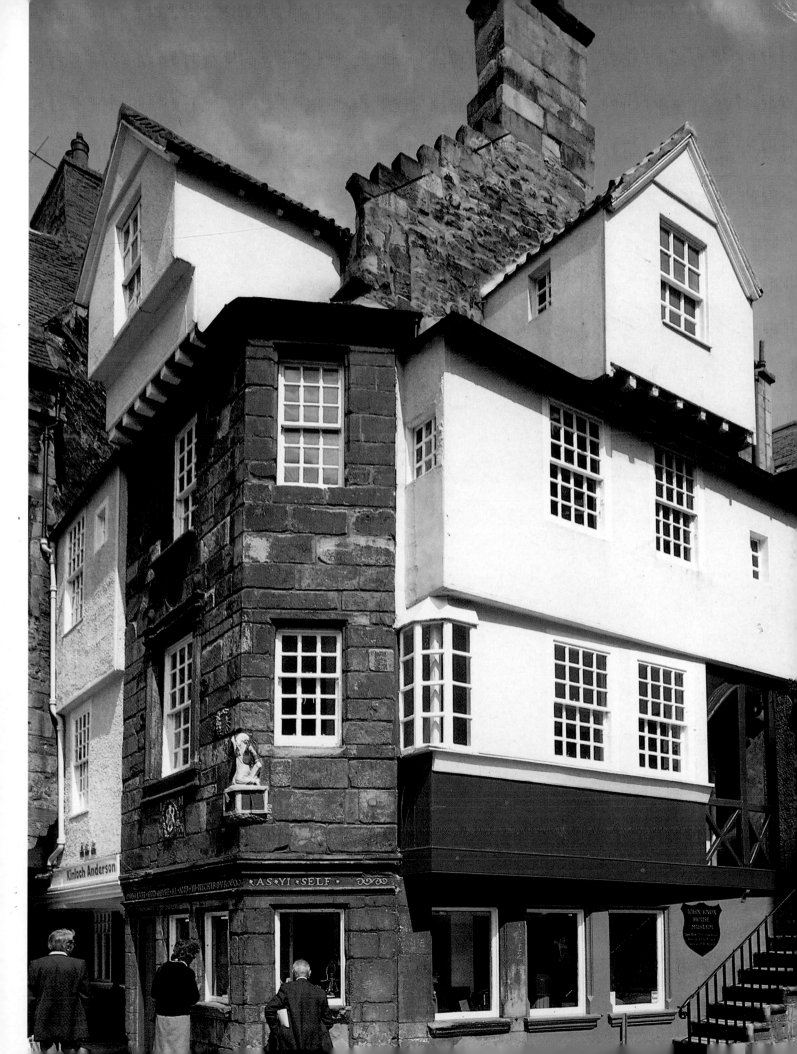

Preceding pages, left: Commanding views of Edinburgh reward those who climb to the top of the Scott Monument, the largest of its kind; it honors poet and novelist Sir Walter Scott. *Right:* John Knox House on Edinburgh's Royal Mile attracts visitors interested in its collection of historical material about the renowned Reformation leader. *This page:* Centuries of history fill the buildings lining High Street, which slopes from Holyrood Palace to Edinburgh Castle. The route is popularly known as the Royal Mile.

Viking settlers made their mark here: They created a mixed heritage that can be heard in some of the island dialects, which are tinged with a Scandinavian accent, and can be seen in the shops, where Norse sweaters are sold instead of tartans.

Scotland's union with England took place less than 300 years ago, in 1707, after hundreds of years of battling. At that time, both Scotland and England dissolved their independent parliaments to create a new parliament of Great Britain. Scotland remains, however, a semi-autonomous country: Scottish banks issue their own notes, although English currency is welcome. And Scotland's legal system is different; it is based on Roman and Germanic law instead of on English Common Law.

With all this in mind, visitors will realize why Scots object to being referred to as English. Scots have a deep sense of national heritage and individualism, and appreciate those who respect that pride.

Scotland's geography provides some clues as to how the country's independent and resourceful culture emerged. For one thing, Scotland shares the same latitude as southern Alaska. Early settlers had to be of hardy mind and body to survive the long, cold winters. As for space, there's plenty of it. Scotland is about twice the size of Switzerland; yet with just over five million people, it has only half the population of its continental neighbor.

Above: Situated on the east end of the Royal Mile is the architecturally distinctive Canongate Tolbooth, which once served as a courthouse, prison, and center of municipal affairs. *Right:* The Royal Mile today remains a center of commercial activity.

The weather in western Scotland is often overcast and wet. Winds blow in from the North Atlantic charged with moisture. Having no coastal mountain range to block their force, storms sweep across the western part of the country, bringing rain, sleet, and snow with them. The western part of the Grampian Mountains, for example, receives more than 100 inches of rain every year on the highest slopes. The eastern side of the country, by contrast, is in a distinct rain shadow, receiving less than 25 inches of rain a year.

Temperatures in Scotland hover in the low to mid 60's in the summer and average in the low 40's in the winter. May and June generally exhibit the best weather, but August and September are also very special months, for that is when the Scottish heather blooms, covering the hillsides with rich shades of pink and purple.

The famous economist, Adam Smith, is buried in the cemetery of Canongate Church. *Below:* Imposing wrought-iron gates form the entrance to the Palace of Holyroodhouse.

This page: Originally built in the early 1500's, the Palace of Holyroodhouse served as a permanent royal residence for little more than a century. It now serves as the residence of Queen Elizabeth II and the Royal Family when they are in Edinburgh. Most of today's palace dates from a major rebuilding that occurred in the late seventeenth century.

This page: The memorial to Scottish philosopher Dugald Stewart (above) shares space on Edinburgh's Calton Hill with the National Monument (below), an unfinished replica of the Parthenon in Athens.

Scotland is divided geologically and economically into three distinct regions: the Highlands, the Central Lowlands, and the Southern Uplands.

The Highlands cover nearly two-thirds of the total area of Scotland, comprising the highest, most barren, and least populated part of Great Britain. Rising in some areas to more than 4,000 feet, most of the terrain of the Highlands consists of the stumps of former mountain ranges created eons ago.

The Central Lowlands region, lower in altitude than both the north and south, has a more hospitable landscape, a wider variety of soils, and a milder climate than elsewhere in the country. It is also the economic and agricultural heartland of Scotland. Scotland's major cities, Edinburgh and Glasgow, are located in the Central Lowlands. Glasgow is to the west on the River Clyde, and Edinburgh is to the east on the northern bank of the Firth of Forth.

Edinburgh is one of the most elegant and civilized capital cities in Europe. It is filled with bookstores, galleries, and museums, and it hosts the largest annual arts festival in the world. The Edinburgh International Festival consists of three weeks of music and theatrical events. Presented simultaneously with the Edinburgh Festival is the Fringe Festival, which is more avant-garde in its offerings. Beginning in late August, the two festivals dominate the city, turning nearly every street corner into a stage.

This page, top to bottom: A copper dome crowning the Bank of Scotland adds color to Edinburgh's skyline. Built to serve travelers arriving by train at adjacent Waverly Station, the North British Hotel is still one of Edinburgh's most notable accommodations. The North Bridge connects the east end of Princes Street in the New Town to the Old Town.

Edinburgh began its days as a tiny settlement on an extinct volcano where the Edinburgh Castle now stands. The city broke out of its small, walled site in the mid-eighteenth century, and it has since expanded to more than 50 square miles. The tone of its early expansion was set by the classical lines of the New Town to the north.

Much of the Old Town still has a medieval flavor, with cobblestone streets that wind around the face of the Castle Rock. The castle itself is rich in Scottish history—names like Mary, Queen of Scots and Prince Charles Edward Stuart (Bonnie Prince Charlie) pepper its past. Over the centuries the castle has served as a fortress, royal palace, treasury, repository of government records, place of worship, and prison.

Today, the castle's windy esplanade features military memorials recalling past glories and disasters. Also on this site sits the Witches' Well, marking the spot where more than 300 women suspected of witchcraft were burned alive between 1479 and 1722.

The Royal Mile is the main road through Edinburgh's Old Town. This road runs westward from the castle to the Palace of Holyroodhouse, an ancient dwelling of the Stuarts, who were the ruling family of Scotland from 1371–1603. Here, more than 100 portraits of Scottish kings line the walls. Many of Edinburgh's oldest houses can be found along the Mile, some dating back to the fifteenth and sixteenth centuries. The principal church of Scotland, the High Kirk of Saint Giles, is also on this route.

This page, top to bottom: Rosslyn Chapel, near the village of Roslin, southeast of Edinburgh, offers a fine example of late medieval stone carving. Scotland's romantic writer, Sir Walter Scott, created Abbotsford House, which today is a museum containing examples of Scott's works and interests. The ruin of Jedburgh Abbey is testament to the centuries of warring that took place at the Scottish-English border.

Above: Culzean Castle in southwest Scotland is an example of architect Robert Adams' remarkable work. *Right:* Toward the end of his life, poet Robert Burns lived in this house in Dumfries that now serves as a museum.

Above, left to right: Once soot-covered, many of Glasgow's buildings and monuments have recently shared in a massive city cleanup. Sir Walter Burrell's impressive art collection was donated to the City of Glasgow and is now housed in an award-winning modern building. The gothic spire of Glasgow University is an impressive 300 feet high. *Below:* The Cathedral of St. Mungo, also known as Glasgow Cathedral, is smaller than many of its kind but is noted for its architecture, which dates to the thirteenth century.

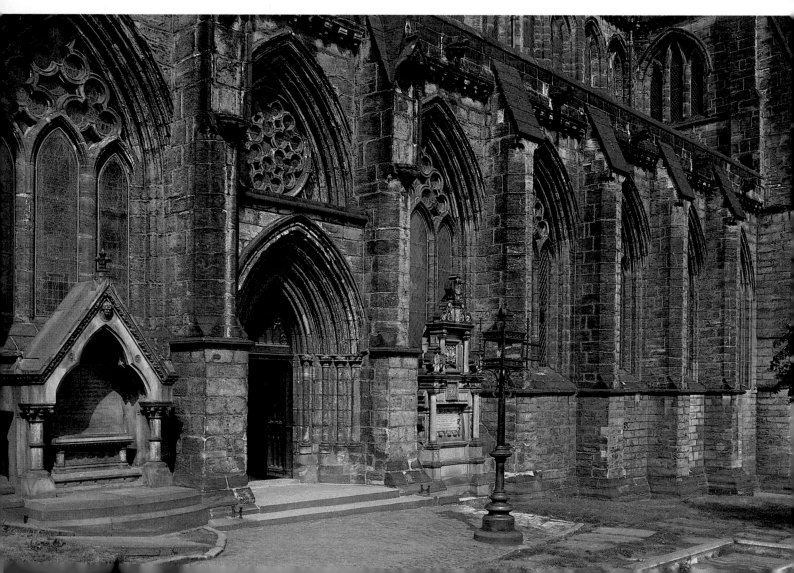

Above: The Italian Renaissance-style Glasgow City Chambers building is guarded by a pair of stalwart stone lions. *Right:* Princes Square, a renovation project involving several Victorian buildings, is a recent addition to Glasgow's shopping district. *Overleaf:* Celebrated in song and folklore, Loch Lomond is 24 miles long, making it the largest freshwater lake in the British Isles.

Greyfriars Kirk and Kirkyard is another historical landmark in the Old Town. This is the site of a Franciscan Friary where the National Covenant was signed in 1638, declaring the Scottish church to be Presbyterian. In keeping with Scotland's dramatic history, many of the names on the National Covenant were signed in blood. Visitors will also find one of Scotland's most extraordinary collections of tombs. Many famous Scots are buried here including the artist, George Jamesone; the Highland poet, Duncan Ban MacIntyre; and John Gray, owner of Greyfriars Bobby (a faithful little dog that is commemorated by a statue).

The New Town, in contrast to the Old Town, is a perfect example of eighteenth-century Georgian architecture. Laid out in a rectangular grid, it encompasses three main parallel streets (Queen, George, and Princes) that link Charlotte and Saint Andrew's Squares, which are lined with elegant Georgian townhouses. Princes Street, now Edinburgh's main shopping district, runs along the north side of the Princes Street Gardens, which sit at the base of the castle.

Leith, the port of Edinburgh, straddles the Water of Leith, which flows into the harbor. This port is rich in history: it was ravaged frequently by the English, as well as visited by welcomed ships carrying the likes of Mary, Queen of Scots, who returned to Scotland in 1561 after spending years in France.

This page: A neat stack of lobster creels (above) sits on the quay in the picturesque fishing village of Crail (left) in East Fife.

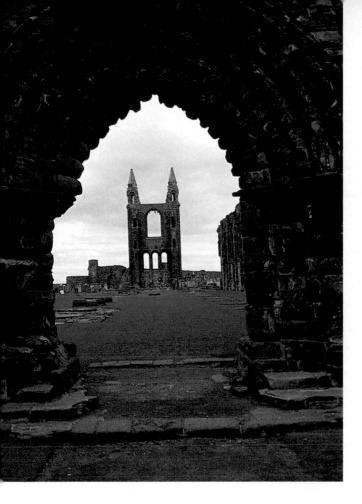

This page: St. Andrews Cathedral was at one time the largest cathedral in Scotland. St. Andrews Castle was the scene of many bloody battles during the sixteenth-century Reformation. The inscriptions on the headstones (below) show that this cemetery continued to be used long after St. Andrews Cathedral fell into ruin.

 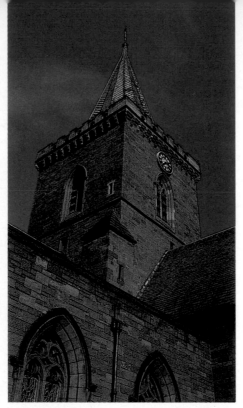 

Above: Now a gallery and crafts shop, The Fair Maid's House in Perth was chosen by Sir Walter Scott as the home of the heroine in his story, *The Fair Maid of Perth.* St. John's Kirk of Perth (center), the site of John Knox's dramatic Reformation sermon, has been restored and maintained since its founding in 1126. Five hundred Highlanders who made up the first regiment of the Black Watch are commemorated in a monument (right) near Aberfeldy in the Tayside region. *Below:* Blair Castle's woodland setting, striking white façade, and fine collection of artifacts make it a popular tourist destination.

Today the harbor consists of a large, open outer expanse of water, and an inner harbor complex of docks—an area that now boasts a fine collection of lively restaurants and pubs.

If Edinburgh has long been elegant and "respectable," then Glasgow is an energetic upstart. For years, most tourists stayed away from Glasgow, considering it a dark industrial city. But recently things have changed. Old buildings are being refurbished, the riverfront is being upgraded, and the arts are growing at such a pace that in 1990 Glasgow was named the European City of Culture.

Mayfest, Glasgow's arts festival, has played a major role in its recent renaissance. Some say this international gathering of musicians, actors, poets, and artists eclipses the Edinburgh Festival, but luckily the festivals are held at different times of the year, so each can be thoroughly enjoyed.

Before Scotland's union with England, Glasgow was a small, beautiful city of about 13,000; it was built around the great medieval Cathedral of Saint Mungo. After the formation of Great Britain, Glasgow became the nation's principal port, harboring ships carrying tobacco imported from the American colonies.

With the rising activity of the port came more jobs, which brought thousands of people to Glasgow. By 1831, the city's population had

This page, top to bottom: Glamis Castle, one of Scotland's largest, boasts a square tower with walls as much as 15 feet thick. The North Sea fishing port of Arbroath is famous for its delicious "smokies," or smoked fish. Dunottar Castle is a sprawling medieval ruin perched precariously on the coast near Aberdeen.

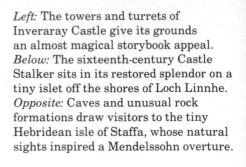

Left: The towers and turrets of Inveraray Castle give its grounds an almost magical storybook appeal. *Below:* The sixteenth-century Castle Stalker sits in its restored splendor on a tiny islet off the shores of Loch Linnhe. *Opposite:* Caves and unusual rock formations draw visitors to the tiny Hebridean isle of Staffa, whose natural sights inspired a Mendelssohn overture.

swelled to 200,000, and by 1840 it was claimed that the quality of life in Glasgow had declined to such an extent that it had become the worst city in Europe in terms of housing and health.

While tobacco was pouring into Britain through Glasgow, goods such as linen, paper, cloth tape, and wrought iron were being manufactured in Scotland to ship to the American colonies. Glasgow's shipbuilding and steel production helped fuel the industrial revolution and by 1861, the city was bursting at the seams. It contained more than 400 thousand people, many of whom had come from Ireland and the Highlands looking for work. Terrible housing, inhumane working conditions, and poor health persisted, eventually arousing the wrath of the working class. Later, Glasgow became a hotbed for social reform, paving the way for improved working conditions and stronger public services.

But shipbuilding and steel production also made some of Glasgow's population very wealthy, and a portion of that wealth went into building a Victorian city grand in both scale and character. Today, tenements built during the Victorian era have been renovated as part of Glasgow's citywide revival efforts.

For those who prefer the countryside, just north of Glasgow the West Highland Way, one of Scotland's longest footpaths, begins. The trail stretches north 95 miles from Scotland's largest city to Great Britain's highest mountain—4,406-foot-high Ben Nevis in the western

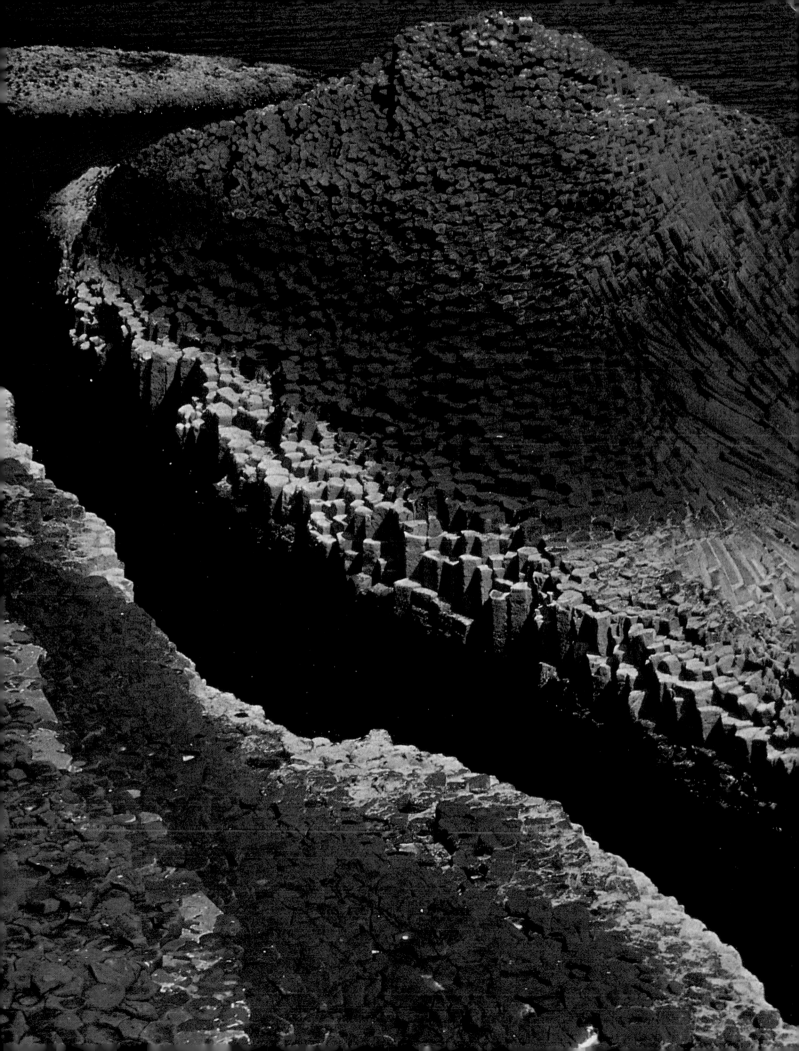

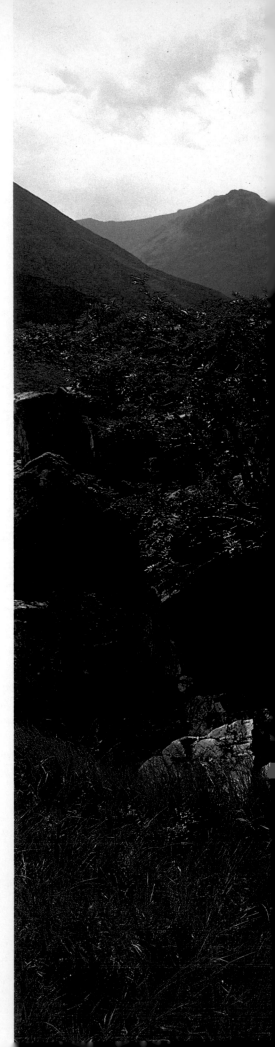

Above: Wild and desolate, Rannoch Moor lies on the edge of the ancient Caledonian forest of the Central Highlands. *Opposite:* Glen Coe is beautiful in its primitive openness, and has understandably become one of Scotland's most appreciated scenic spots.

Above: The West Highland Railway Line passes spectacular scenery, including monolithic Beinn Doran, on its route between Glasgow, Fort William, and Mallaig. *Left:* These hearty Highland cattle are well suited to the rigors of the northern Scotland climate. *Opposite:* Rugged terrain and political hardships have created a sparse and scattered population in the Scottish Highlands.

Grampian Mountains. Numerous lochs (lakes) can be found in this region, as well as the headwaters of several such notable rivers as the Tay, the Earn, and the Forth. Hiking and bicycling are very popular in this area, but fanciers of these activities usually encounter a little drizzle.

The Scottish Lowlands (Southern Uplands) lie north of England's border. The majority of the landscape here is a crazy quilt of forest and barren moorland, with picturesque villages and castles scattered throughout the region.

Scotland's longest hillwalk, the Southern Upland Way, is also located here. It runs 212 miles from the harbor town of Portpatrick on the southwest coast to Cockburnspath, about 30 miles east of Edinburgh. Like its northern counterpart, the West Highland Way, the long-distance footpath is well marked and maintained by Britain's Countryside Commission. Comprising a variety of lanes, paths, and trails, this walk passes through towns, along highways, up hills, and across forests.

In the southwest corner of Scotland is the region known as Ayrshire. The Scottish bard, Robert Burns, was born in the village of Alloway, two miles south of the popular resort town of Ayr. Burns' Cottage is here, as well as a multimedia center detailing the poet's life and times. Every June, Ayr hosts the Ayrshire Arts Festival, which coincides with the Robert Burns Festival. Both offer music and verse by the "poet of the people," along with a wide spectrum of dance and drama.

Above: The much-photographed, twelfth-century Eilean Donan Castle in Dornie guards the entrance to three west coast sea lochs. *Left:* To the north sits the village of Ploekton on the shore of Loch Carron.

At one time one of the largest castles in Scotland, the ruins of Castle Urquhart sit on the shore of Loch Ness. *Below:* Since the seventeenth century there have been reports of a mysterious creature living in the deep, dark waters of Loch Ness.

South of Ayr is Culzean Castle, built from 1772 to 1792 by the famous Scottish architect Robert Adam. The castle sits on a coastal cliff, surrounded by beautiful grounds that extend to 563 acres. Many think the castle's interior contains some of the architect's best work; it includes an oval staircase and a round drawing room. Once the retreat of the Scottish Kennedy's, the castle and park are now part of Britain's National Trust, which has opened it up to the public.

In general, southern Scotland has a gentle feel to it. Popularly known as the "quiet country," the Scots accent is milder here than in the central and northern regions. The region's topography also reflects this pastoral nature in its moderate hills and miles of flat grasslands. But, like the rest of the country, the south has a long, romantic, and bloody history, giving visitors much to see and do when touring its villages.

Heading westward to the coast, travelers should be prepared for a sharp contrast in scenery. Here, the rough waters of the North Atlantic cut into the coastline, creating fiords with dramatic sea stacks. A visit to Cape Wrath provides even more drama, as the northernmost tip of the western shore reveals giant waves crashing against the highest sea cliffs in mainland Britain.

Above: Culloden House near Inverness boasts an impressive sandstone façade. *Left:* A memorial marks the site of Culloden Moor, where an army led by Bonnie Prince Charlie was defeated in 1746 in the last Scottish-English battle to be fought on British soil. *Opposite:* After his army was defeated at Culloden, Prince Charles escaped to the Isle of Skye, where he was aided by Flora MacDonald, who is commemorated in this statue in Inverness.

Preceding page: Dramatic coastline and a variety of sea birds can be seen by those who follow the footpath above the Bullers of Buchan in northeast Scotland. *This page:* Cruden Bay has recently become the site of oil exploration, but it still holds a link to its fishing past. *Below:* Seaside villages like Pennan have changed very little through the years.

Scotland's east coast is much more gentle in appearance. The Grampian Mountain region, north of Aberdeen, boasts 100 miles of sandy beaches. Sea cliffs also run along this stretch of coast; although they are not as high as the west coast cliffs, they are dramatic for their sheer vertical drop. There is an added bonus—70 castles and a dozen or more distilleries are scattered throughout the area.

One of the most notable people to build a castle in this region was Queen Victoria. She and Prince Albert purchased an estate in Aberdeenshire where an old castle, built in 1484, stood in ruins. They tore it down and built Balmoral Castle in the mid 1800's, using local granite and decorating it with different plaids. As a result of the Queen's love for tartan, the pattern became the most fashionable cloth of the Victorian age.

Another old estate is Craigievar Castle, near the town of Alford. Built in the early 1600's by William Forbes, an Aberdeen merchant, this castle is known for its Scottish baronial architecture. The structure is granite and has an elaborate roof-line of turrets and cupolas. Inside, the castle features remarkable ceiling plasterwork.

Yet another distinguished estate is Crathes Castle, near the town of Banchory. This castle was built in the late sixteenth century and contains fine painted ceilings of that period. The estate also has six acres of walled gardens, subdivided by tall hedges that were planted in 1702.

This page, top to bottom: Barley grown in the Grampian region is harvested for use in the whiskey industry. Distilleries dot the "Whiskey Trail" from Rothes to Tomintol to Huntly. After the barley has ripened to a golden brown, it is distilled into Scotch whiskey and aged in oak barrels for at least two years.

Above: The ruin of Huntly Castle (left) in the Grampian region is noted for its sizeable dungeon, which can be reached by visitors who dare to enter its dark and forbidding passage. Crathes Castle (center) has eight beautiful gardens and exceptional architectural detail. While many Scottish castles have been destroyed or altered, Craigievar (right) has remained virtually unchanged since its completion in 1626. *Below:* For 650 years, until as recently as 1976, Drum Castle was owned by the de Irwin family; it is now in the care of the National Trust for Scotland.

Preceding pages, left: The tumbling waters of the River Dee are forced through a narrow gorge at the Linn of Dee, a popular picnic site. *Right:* A setting sun silhouettes the granite tower of Marischal College, now part of the University of Aberdeen. *This page:* Aberdeen is an important seaport. It serves the North Sea oil industry and is home to Scotland's largest fishing fleet.

Above: A statue in Aberdeen (left) commemorates William Wallace, a thirteenth-century Scottish warrior who led fierce rebellions against the English. Aberdeen also honors Robert Burns in a tribute (right) to this Scottish literary legend, one of many such tributes throughout the city. *Below:* A unicorn sits atop Aberdeen's Mercat Cross in the heart of the city's commercial district.

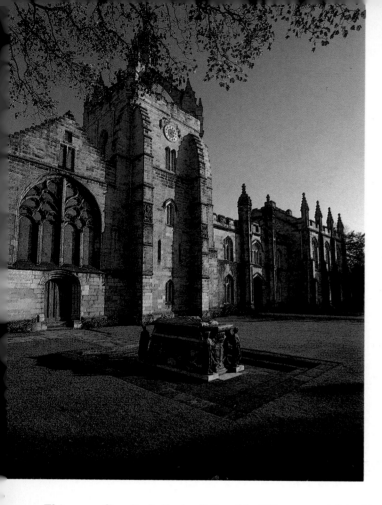

This page: Granite is the traditional building material in Aberdeen, giving the city the name Granite City. The stone lends a clean and solid appearance to the fine antique structures in distinctive Old Aberdeen. Old Aberdeen was once a separate town but is now part of the City of Aberdeen.

This page: Every year on the first Saturday in September, dancers, pipers, and athletes assemble for the Braemar Royal Highland Gathering on Deeside. The day of festivities and competition attracts determined strongmen, who form tug-of-war teams representing distilleries and other workplaces.

After years of neglect, Raasay House, on the Island of Raasay off the east coast of Skye, has found new life as an Outdoor Education Center. *Below:* Formidable Dunvegan Castle on the Isle of Skye is the ancestral home of Clan MacLeod.

All year round, hikers and climbers find plenty of challenges on Skye's jagged spine of mountains, the Cuillins; on clear days the Cuillins offer wonderful views of Hebridean scenery. *Below:* A desolate burial ground on Skye moorland illustrates how forbidding this island can be.

On the Hebridean Isle of Harris are several magnificent prehistoric sites, including the Standing Stones of Callanish, considered one of the most significant of such sites in the British Isles.

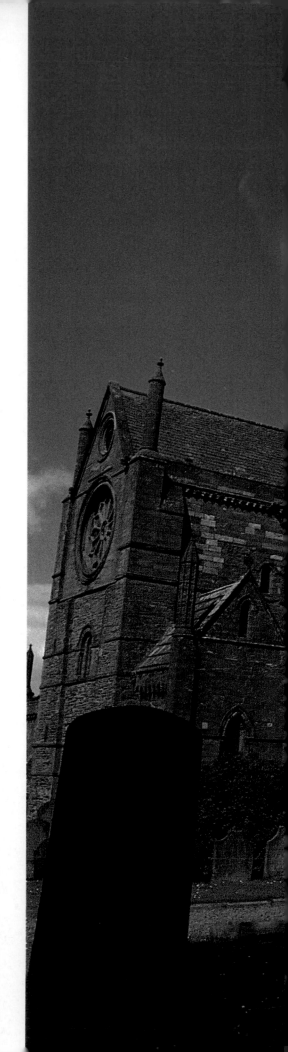

Above: Iron and brick exquisitely detail the bulky form of St. Magnus Cathedral on mainland Orkney Island.
Opposite: The immense cross shape of St. Magnus Cathedral houses tombs of both its founder, St. Magnus, and its patron saint, St. Rognvald.

The island of Lewis is the largest in the Outer Hebrides chain. Here, the landscape is barren, characterized by miles and miles of flat moorland. Crofts (small farms) are widespread, and there are a number of well-preserved ruins dating back to a medieval Celtic civilization.

Scotland boasts scenic variety that ranges from pastoral lands in the Lowlands to the mountains in the northwest Highlands that pile up to a wild and fretted coast. In addition to its stunning scenery and rich history, Scotland is full of friendly people who love to tell stories about this colorful country.

People from all over the world come to Scotland to climb its mountains, boat across its lochs, wander its extensive footpaths, and take in its many festivals. The famous "Scottish mist" is often with visitors as they enjoy the countryside, but that is part of its charm. Pubs and restaurants are where the locals meet, and provide guests with shelter from the elements. A strong pint of beer, Scottish salmon, and even haggis await patrons in many of these havens. And visitors should try them all, for nowhere will they taste quite as good as in the country that is known for its hearty food and cheerful people.

This page, top to bottom: Stacked bales of hay form an abstract design as they dry in the sun on an Orkney farm. Stone, including flagstone for roofing, is a common building material on the almost timberless Orkneys. The Orkney Islands contain Britain's largest collection of prehistoric relics, including Skara Brae, a Stone Age settlement dating to approximately 3,000 B.C.

Above: The ruins of seventeenth-century Earl Patrick's Castle (left) dominate the fishing harbor of Scalloway (right) in the Shetland Isles off Scotland's north coast. *Below:* Each January the streets of the Shetland Isles' capital, Lerwick, on Mainland, Shetland's largest island, come alive with "Up Helly Aa," an ancient festival celebrating the Shetlands' Norse heritage.

Crofting – a type of subsistence farming – continues to this day in Shetland. *Below:* Peat used for heating and cooking is laid out to dry on the Island of Harris in the Outer Hebrides. *Opposite:* The cliffs of Esha Ness on the western Shetland Isles are home to many sea birds. *Overleaf:* Far out in the Atlantic, separate from other Shetland islands, is tiny Foula, with its 1,200-foot cliffs.

Index of Photography

All photographs courtesy of The Image Bank, except where indicated *.